TO KILL ANOTHER HUMAN BEING JUST TO GET
A REPUTATION IS NOT GANGSTER,
IT IS NOT COOL… IT IS PURE IGNORANCE!

IF YOU TRULY SEE YOURSELF AS A MAN
TREAT OTHERS WITH RESPECT. BE
MAN ENOUGH TO KEEP THE PEACE AND SAVE
A LIFE INSTEAD OF TAKING ONE.
IF YOU CAN DO THAT; IN MY BOOK I SAY THAT
IS GANGSTER!

My words are written from my heart I do not expect for everyone to like what I write or how I express myself really what else is new I am prepared for the criticism and all the other nonsense to come just know what thing I write because I love to write and I know that there are people out there who will appreciate my words like and love my words and I believe somewhere with all the different things I write about my words may even help people I have learned a lot over the years made some mistakes and poor choices suffered some consequences I wish I did not have too but I will say this the best thing that any human being in this world can do is be respectful learn to love rather than to hate stop judging others by the way they look, by the car they drive or how much money one may have because when the day comes for that person to be buried they cannot take any of what they may once had on earth with them no man or woman is better than the next we all fall short I will never fear a person because of what they have or who they think they maybe for the simple fact no human being on earth is wiser nor stronger than Jehovah God.

To Women All Over The World:

Never let a man tell you, you are nothing without him truth is he is nothing without you;

Do not allow yourself to become a door mat or a punching bag;

Respect yourself and stand strong let your mind express your natural beauty rather than derogative clothing;

If you a single parent mother and you holding it down I commend you and trust me God is watching over you and blessings will be sent your way;

Don't beat yourself up about poor choices and mistakes you made and damn sure don't let some foul ass man hold them against you because more than likely he will find a way to manipulate you with your past and that is not right;

Never let a man have control over your mind and body more than likely when someone is trying to control you they are weak and afraid of something or just don't know how to be an appropriate man;

Life is too short for you beautiful women to be stressed out so have fun enjoy life appreciate it its God's greatest gift and he wants you to cherish it in the right way every moment.

Ladies you have it hard enough this I know for sure so at least we men can do is respect you because without you there would be no men in the first place I seen how hard things were for not only my mother but many women and you deserve better but as I said hold on to God and things will be alright.

I respect the women of the world

Drugs, Disease and Sex

Do you remember what happened Last Night?

Yesterday was a bad day for you, I understand how it is I been there before but the thing is we should not want to repeat this kind of behavior.

The alcohol and drugs are destroying your beautiful spirit, mind and body the loving, kind intelligent person you once were is no longer there the alcohol and cocaine has chased that side of you away.

When I try to help you, all we do is argue fuss and fight I wonder if you even remember what happened last night.

Last night I had to come get you from another place I don't really care to talk about at all, our love was once true but now it seems as if it's just one big lie, so many nights I have gone for long walks or drives asking God to help you kick this habit of drugs and alcohol.

Last night you stole your mothers jewelry and sold it for drugs you were so drunk you attacked your own child you disrespected me and left the house and we have been searching for you all night only to find you here it's time for you to get help or we have no choice but to turn away from you the family will no longer go through this pain of you slowly killing yourself.

We will do anything to help you if you are serious but you have to be for real just look at your children they need you in their life so don't ruin their lives because of your alcohol and drug abuse if you get it together they will be alright but only you can make that happen.

As I talk to you, you appear to be confused you try to put things together but you really don't remember what happened last night.

What's my name?

I can make you feel good, but if you abuse me too much I will make you feel pain honestly you will love me I will make you do things for me you never thought you would if you treat me wrong I will do my best to make sure you suffer it's a shame the power I can have over a person so many people want me I don't go out and look for them they come looking for me so don't blame me for what they do just tell me what is my name?

Be careful how you handle me I can be very dangerous and hideous to one's life I have the power to make you kill and steal for me once you fall in love with me you would lose your mind over me and beat someone over the head for me, end up in jail or even get killed fighting over me I would have you so hooked you would not care you'll be so open off of me you would steal from your mama.

Are you a weak man because I can take all of your money at the blink of an eye are you a woman with a low self-esteem because I will have you tricking for me break you down until you are in the pit of hell.

I have been known to make mothers and fathers sell their soul for me I told you I am powerful I am that Bitch for real so warn your sons and daughters about me because I am heartless.

Drug dealers have lost their freedom and lives for me I am very bad so naughty I come in two colors can you guess which one's ha-ha either way it don't matter I hurt you all the same what's sad is you chose me I never choose you just tell me what's my name.

I will have you tripping off of me so bad your friends and family would turn they back on you I can make you get to the point you will lose your job, car, house and all your hard earned money because you to busy hooked on me chasing my sexy ass around I'm telling you mess with me if you dare I bet your life you never met a nasty bitch like me you still don't know my name the pleasure is all mind I am crack-cocaine

DAD LOVES CRACK MORE THAN ME

My father's drug habit is out of control
Crack has him chained down stuck deep in a hole
Because of his drug abuse and neglect to the family
We don't spend time together anymore, because he's out
Tricking on some slut getting high.

I remember when my dad used to be a peaceful loving family man then
he brought crack into our lives ever since then we've had nothing but
pain and broken promises of him going to get help so he can kick this
habit crack is a deadly monster.

Dad I miss the times we shared hanging out at the park playing ball you
educating me on the do's and don'ts of life. I wish you could see how
your addiction is killing you and destroy your family.

The life you are living is truly heart aching and disgusting it's like all
you do is eat, sleep, and shit crack
You're the drug dealer's number one Fein. What happened to never
letting negativity come between us?

Sure is amazing how my DAD LOVES CRACK MORE THAN
ME!

How long will it be until you wake up and realize right from wrong day
after day I pray God once again makes you strong so you can do the
right things as you're supposed to.

How long will it take for you to clean up your life?

Have you forgotten about your children and beautiful loyal loving wife?

Because little do you know just like you lost your job you're going to lose your family, closest friends and all the great things you worked so hard for.

I pray and pray until my eyes can cry no more wondering why My DAD LOVES CRACK MORE THAN ME!

Temptation:

Drug dealers offer me sweet bitter packages to move tempting me to get back in the mix only if they knew the pain I felt from pushing twenties dimes and nicks I don't have time for the negativity.

Lord you are my fortress redemption and salvation;

Please father is my shield and my protection without you I am nothing but with you I am somebody. I once was addicted to selling drugs and other kinds of negative living but because of you Lord I have overcome that there's no way I can fall back into that cold dark hole walk with me Lord.

I pray for my brothers and sisters who are caught in the struggle living in satins world I pray God blesses you with the proper strength to turn away from evil ways of living because life is the most beautiful gift that God has ever given us.

I was one who used to lie, cheat, steal, and destroy lives, quick to beat on a person for that dirty green dollar the drug game made me an animal I became a monster I never wanted to be.
But one day God showed me I wasn't the roughest cat in the street I nearly lost my life, was I ever really a thug no just a follower who got caught up in a fowl circle that looked good
But it's like they say everything that glitters is not gold.

Now I am a true example that God is good he saved me many times although I felt some pain he still came to my rescue took me out of satins world brought me back into his house so safe and warm.

I know that if my life was left in man's hands I would either be dead or in prison for a very long time but because of God's love kindness and mercy my life is in his hands there's a purpose for me sharing my story and a reason why I wake up every day giving God all the Glory.

DRUGS KILLED MOM AND DAD

Today I live without a mother or father

But I do have my grandmother to look after me this

Hurts so bad I am only eleven years old and my world

Is so gloomy and cold

God please forgive my parents for the terrible things

They have done I know they never meant to do the horrible

Crimes and sell their souls to satin for crack but that habit is so

Bad and once it has you it stops at nothing to destroy you

And majority of people who do get caught out there end up

Struggling or dead.

I just want to tell all parents that drugs are dangerous drugs

Kill, steal and destroy another form of the devil before my parents

Got strung out on crack we used to have the best family life

Home was truly a home that is until my parents smoked away

Our beautiful home then from there were living in hotels,

Sleeping at friends and families houses sometimes barely eating

Oh but mom and dad they stayed high all the time.

Is there anyone out there who feels my pain I need answers some body

Please explain to me how crack came into existence, through my parents

I have learned what drugs can do to one's soul that's why I state my

Word never to sell myself shorts for a quick fix and get caught up in the mix

Running with brothers up to no good feigning for tricks letting crack come

Between my children, and me close family members and friends.

I pray for strength please God pull me through this storm

Take away my pain let the sun come out and shine and chase

Away the rain people wonder why I walk around so sad because

Drugs killed mom and dad.

FOR THE MOTHERS WHO ARE STRUGGLING:

A child sits alone in the kitchen crying in the dark trying hard to block out the noise ignoring the fact that his mother is in the room selling herself for some good old china white never giving thought about the damage she is doing to her beautiful child, that's not right at all.

She doesn't realize his hurt or even that she is destroying herself because getting high is the only thing on her mind, now the young boy starts to see mama is fiend a slut for drugs he sees that mama can't keep a job or a good man in her life he begins to lose respect for his mama and this is the worst thing that can happen when your own child no longer sees his sweet mama he now looks at another crack head.

My words may seem cruel and bitter and I do apologize but my Beautiful sisters I just want you to open up your spirits, minds and hearts and put those drugs down and understand that your children need you, that your families need you, and that man who loves you needs you as well.

Ladies I know it's hard at times to raise the child or children especially when you have to do it all alone but drugs is not the solution, don't stress that dad is a dead beat a sucker that won't do his part its ok if you got more heart than him.

Remember that your child needs you more than any one so just have faith pray for strength, guidance and courage and always pray and know that GOD does and will answer you turn your lives around to a positive way so that your sons or daughters can say wow when I grow up that's how I want to be successful, strong, smart and full of courage.

I'M DYING:

I am 20 years old and my life has been cut short I didn't take this serious didn't think it could happen to me, so instead of a suit for graduation my parents are down at the mall looking for a suit to bury me in so much pain and suffering I have caused not only myself but my loved as well no smiles just tears.

When the doctor told me I had full blown Aides I wanted to die right then and there, I am not sure how I got or which partner either because I lived a life of shooting dope and dysfunctional sex of female and male unprotected.

Please pay close attention to me because I am your prime example of stupidity of what drugs and sex can do to a person look how by not doing the right thing I robbed myself of a happy life.

If I could do it all over again I definitely would not bring drugs into my life and if I did have sex it would be with one person protected or wait until I am married which is the best thing and GOD does honor such good things.

This is the price I had to pay because I wanted to play with drugs and sex and disobeyed GOD'S instructions so I say to my brothers and sisters as well turn away from your negative ways before you end up like me 20 years old begging for forgiveness and mercy trying to make the best out of my last days.

MAMA YOU'R
KILLING ME:

She sits in her room with so much hurt, anger and eyes full of tears trying to understand why mama is with those people getting high down stairs.

Nowhere to run or hide she's lost her soul no more pride and mama can't see because she's too busy smoking crack pleasing her wicked flesh being so selfish.

Mama your killing me is what she screams out in her room begging God for help to take the pain away and free her mother from the belly of the beast because her drug habit is slowly destroying their lives it's just not fair that mama no longer cares about who and what is important.

Life and love is a blessing from GOD so one should not throw it away on negativity. What joy does one get out of smoking crack? What is so good about going to rehabs and losing your job, house, money, car and family just for one hit off that shiny glass dick. If you stop and think about it does it really make.

Mama my sweet mama and to all the mothers in the world please stop killing your selves before it's too late, Mama what must I do to show you that I love you I guess our bond as mother and daughter is not enough so should I start smoking crack also just so we can communicate mama you just don't understand your killing me.

OVER DOSE:

I did not think it would happen to me, but I guess I was wrong never did I think that cocaine would put me in the hospital I had my habit under control. Man was I wrong and this is why now I lay here with tubes up my nose I.V. dripping into my body and my stomach is being pumped as if it were a sewer backed up.

Getting high off of this shit has caused me to fall into the pit of hell my entire life at this point is going nowhere, but cocaine sweet cocaine you was there for me whenever I needed you especially when the chips were down so how could you do this to me.

No I must not look for excuses it's time to let go of this deadly drug and move into a positive direction with my life GOD help me speak to me please make a way for me because I don't want to die and truly not like this.

I am tired of letting myself down and my family as well so GOD I put my life in your hands I need you to rescue me from this dark world not only me but my brothers and sisters also because right about now we are blind all we see is that white sexy devil called cocaine please FATHER save me from this overdose.

TWO YEARS CLEAN:

It's been two years since I last used drugs I think about how hard I had to fight my cocaine addiction it was a hard fight but today I can honestly say I feel good and I thank GOD for giving me the strength to kick such a wicked habit.

Drugs ruled my life for so many years my heart endured so much pain my eyes shed so many tears, bringing shame on myself and my family. I stole from loved ones, robbed houses, stores old people and young I didn't give a fuck about human life all I wanted to do was get high so forgive me if I seem so happy I got every right to be I have two years clean.

I 'm not here to tell you how to run your life I just know how sniffing cocaine ruined my life how it stripped me of a good job beautiful wife and child. So please take my advice and leave that poison alone before it destroys all that you stand for don't be like me and find out the hard way and then have to start all over again listen to my words and save you're self-save a loved one or friend.

You will never know how good I feel to be able to look in the mirror and see that I am not that evil monster any more
Now today instead of searching for the next high I give God all the glory and share with you my story and pray that just like me you will have two years clean.

MOMMY I'M HUNGRY

Your child is hungry and you're not around to feed him that's because you are too busy running the streets getting high having so-call fun with so-call friends neglecting your beautiful son, what kind of mother are you? How does that make you feel to know your child is starving and it's your fault?

Weak after weak you say you are going to do better and do what is right but nothing has yet changed you lie to yourself and your child. What's it going to take for you to wake up and be a mother when social services come get him I know you heard him last name crying out mommy I am HUNGRY…?

Mothers like you give good mothers a bad name don't blame on the father you knew he was a dead beat from the start so step up to the plate and love your child the right way.

Your ways are disgusting and shameful let me ask you a question how would you feel if you were being treated this way and if you have then you should understand the hurt your very own is going through I pray to GOD mothers like you straighten up and open your eyes it's not fair for that young boy to be screaming MOMMY I'M HUNGRY…

SECTION II:

ENCOURAGEMENT

FOR THE LADIES:

Ladies when your man leaves you and your child don't stress because he was just a loser any way don't worry that he slid off with that other chick because he was just holding you back stopping you from shining just know that GOD WILL PULL YOU THROUGH so do not be afraid nor lose your faith.

Sweet lady you can be anything you choose you don't need that punk to make you ask yourself what is really doing for you go out there and become that lawyer, doctor, actress, top model, nurse or millionaire. Any man who does not want his woman to succeed is a weak man and nine times out of ten does not want anything for himself as well.

Life is too short ladies to just settle for less its either you go for the gusto or nothing at all why settle for a hot dog when you can have steak get out in the world and do what you must in order to have a happy life.

I am talking to all women all over the world so take heed to my words you don't have to sit there and get beat down spiritually, mentally or physically by some sucker do you ma shine like the stars.

Make that cat respect you be strong and let him know you are intelligent you have a heart and it deserves to be loved in the right way show that dude you are a real lady not some chicken looking for an easy way out just wanting to lay up get fucked and smoke weed all day no let him know you are the real deal because the younger girls are looking up to you so don't let them down.

It's Up To Us

This our neighborhood so let's keep it safe and clean for the children if we don't care who will care at all about our environment and our children if we show each other love our children will know how to show and give love.

So when you see a child doing something wrong do not be afraid to speak up and pull that youngster to the side and drop a lifesaving jewel on him or her there's nothing wrong with encouraging our youth to be better than us to live right and be smart.

We have the power to protect our streets so why not I mean this is where we live its only right that we live in peace without worry of guns, drugs and violence as well but it's up to us to make the change let's not please the enemy by destroying our community and each other instead let us not only build up our community but les us build each other up and not bring harm on one another I don't know about you but I love my black brothers and sisters and I am tires of seeing us beat each other down.

Who is going to truly teach our children the real history of the black struggle and tell them the truth from beginning to end its up to us who is going to teach them how drugs, gangs, guns, violence and other criminal acts is what has also held us captive for far too long.

I want the youth of today to know that the bad things we did or that they may see now is not cool but what is cool is getting an education and learning to be a mature responsible respectful person is cool there's too many youth going to prison and dying at a young age because they are not being taught how to live life wisely so I say to all the real men and women it's up to us to teach our youth and show them the way.

LIFE SAVER:

You rescued me when I was in danger;
You kept me from wondering off with that evil stranger;
You humbled me when I was filled with anger;
You blessed me with good morals, taught that it is better to love
then to hate.
This is why I can say you are my life saver…

When I talk about life saver I am not talking about some kind of
sweet candy no I am talking about my heavenly father because all
the things he has done for me has been nothing but his sweet love
and only GOD could have done all the good things I have been
blessed with.

You are with me everywhere I go
Your word is always the truth
Your love, kindness and chastisement is living proof
You are my life saver…

You are my light that shines through the deepest darkness
I am yours and you are mine
I believe in your son I believe in you
You are my life saver……

Thank you GOD for having mercy on me
And forgiving me for my sins.

TIME FOR A CHANGE:

I have lived this negative life for far too long and all that I had I eventually lost, the only thing I have to show for it is nightmares, scars and time lost locked behind bars.

I've seen so many men drop never ending tears because they are about to climb the mountains for the next 50 years of their life, who really wants to live a life like this. How can any man expect to hold his family down sitting behind the wall trapped in the belly of the beast this is not the way to live?

When it comes to selling drugs none of us are winners no matter how much money you may be making, no matter how slick you think you are by paying off the police, fiends, snakes, snitches and those so called hood niggers who are really scared of their own shadow GOD has a way of putting an end to all of us who sin.

I remember how I used to be surrounded by the finest females, top notch gangsters and rollers, and all those who would beg, borrow, steal and kill to either A. be down on my team B. Buy my drugs or C. just simply do whatever I ordered them to do. Yeah it's a dirty game but somebody has to play it it's a shame what money, power, woman and drugs can do to one's soul how easy it can take over your mind.

The streets changed me from a Good loyal man to an evil, selfish, dishonest person which caused me to lose all the greatest things in my life such as family, friends and the only woman that truly loved me.

So today I tell you my story I hope that you take heed to my words so many nights I have got down on my knees crying out to GOD for mercy and forgiveness asking for strength to live a positive peaceful life because deep in my heart I know it's time for a change.

USE YOUR MIND FOR YOU AND NOT AGAINST YOU!

IF WE CAN GET LITTLE POCKETS OF SAFETY WE CAN GROW!

BEING IN SAFETY MAKES ONE FEEL GOOD!

ON A TWO WAY STREET YOU HAVE A CHOICE BUT ON A ONE WAY STREET YOU HAVE NONE!

HURT, PAIN, AND MISERY IS A CHOICE WE DO NOT HAVE TO MAKE!

WE EITHER TEACH OURSELVES TO SUCCEED OR FAIL! WHAT ARE YOU TEACHING YOURSELF?

THE PATH OF PEACE IS FULL OF LIFE BUT THE PATH OF VIOLENCE ENDS IT, SO WHICH ONE WILL YOU CHOOSE?

<u>Love My Brother</u>

We have laughed, fought and argued but still I love my brother

We don't always agree but still I love you brother

We have always been there for each other no matter the situation good, bad wrong or right even if it was other's we had to fight its all good because I love my brother

When you cry I cry when you smile I smile because I love my brother

Some may never understand the bond we have because we are true brothers real brothers who will always hold one another down you are my brother and I love you.

6.7 Million PEOPLE IN CORRECTIONAL FACILITIES.

2 MILLION PEOPLE ARE IN PRISON

4 BILLION ON PROBATION.

7 MILLION ON PAROLE.

DON'T BE A PART OF THIS EVIL SYSTEM

THE YOUNGEST TEENAGER IN JAIL IS 16 YEARS OLD.

85% OF TEENAGERS IN JAIL ALREADY HAVE BEEN
ARRESTED WITHIN ONE YEAR END UP
GOING BACK TO JAIL BEFORE THE END OF THE FIRST YEAR.

PRISON IS PREDJUDICE TO NONE, BUT THE ODDS ARE
STACKED MORE ON THE POOR. DUE TO LACK OF FUNDS THE
GOVERNMENT, KNOWS LOW INCOME FAMILIES CANNOT
AFFORD TO BAIL THEIR LOVED ONE'S OUT OF JAIL OR
AFFORD AN ATTORNEY.

The Woman:

She is beautiful

She is intelligent

She is strong

She is respectful

She is the one who loves you

She will make sacrifices put you first and herself last

She will cry for you and smile for you

She will encourage you to be the best man you can possibly be!

So don't take advantage of her love and abuse her mentally or physically because you are too weak to handle such a real woman like her. Who gives you or any man the right to call her a bitch and put your hands or her, It does not matter what the situation is she is female there's ways to address an issue with a woman without getting ignorant calling her names and putting your hands on her The same way God created you he created the woman as well and he does not want any of his beautiful creations to be abused mentally or physically so remember the next time you see yourself about to get into an altercation with your woman look into her eyes and see how beautiful she is and be man enough to walk away the woman was created for us to love protect and honor and encourage her to be phenomenal every day of her life.

To my brothers:

I remember how I used to sell cocaine and crack to my people and was quick to beat a cat down for my money smack a female if she wasn't doing her job as told yeah I learned a lot out of living that life style I remember how I got stabbed and how I went to jail and how in the end I was a loser.

Little hustler you think you coming up off them grams you weak young man your mind is twisted that's not your grind your fronting out on them streets trying to be somebody you're not.

You wasting time smoking weed getting drunk selling crack while time is passing you by oh I forgot you can't realize it your too busy getting high living fairytales your entire life is a fucking lie you a nickel and dime hustler a broke ass buster what's good with you.

Are you selling the drugs because to me it looks like the drugs are selling you I 'm not trying to preach I just know what happens to one when he chooses the wrong path it's never a happy ending to this story.

Not a Good Look

Pants sagging draws showing cursing talking slang showing no respect for yourself or others what kind of role model are you being to your brothers and this is how you express yourself to your sisters this is now how a man represents himself.

You want a job but your too hood to hold one down you want a real mature woman but your too childish to handle a real lady because you still think it's all about smoking piff and getting drunk telling lies and playing games.

Don't hate on the man who knows how to dress properly has an education and works hard for his, who speaks without using slang and is respected by many nah don't hate instead learn something from the one who is being a positive example.

I am not trying to disrespect you I am enlighten you on your behavior because the mentality you possess at this point is not healthy if I ask you where do you see yourself in five years what would tell me don't answer just think about it.

If you want to be successful you have to think, walk, talk and present yourself as success being hood does not bring you success its cool to wear what you want but just be appropriate if you came to my door looking a mess I would feel some kind of way and pardon for judging but first time impression means everything.

Hanging on the corner throw up gang signs not caring about yourself destroying the community with drugs and violence is not cool no not at all what you are doing my brother is not a good look.

BE YOUR BEST FRIEND
NOT YOU'RE WORST ENEMY!

A REAL MAN WILL CHOOSE PEACE!

NEVER BE AFRAID TO ASK FOR HELP!

BE INSPIRED TO LEARN!

MAKE THE RIGHT CHOICE AND TAKE VIOLENCE OUT OF
YOUR LIFE!

SAYING NO TO KNOWLEDGE IS SAYING NO TO LIFE!

WITH NO EDUCATION YOU REMAIN IN DEGRADATION!

HOW ARE YOU PREPARING YOUR SELF FOR MANHOOD?

JUST LOOK AROUND
THE STREET MENTALITY ONLY KEEPS YOU DOWN, WILL
YOU RISE ABOVE IT?

WHEN THE SUNRISES:

I pray that the leaders of countries will stop fighting and put an end to all war

A cure for Aides, Cancer and other deadly diseases will be found

Gang violence will die and my brothers and sisters will began to live

I also pray fathers will become positive role models to their children and step into their lives on a full time basis

Mothers as well will become fine examples to their daughters and sons instead neglecting them

My brothers will see that there is no future in selling drugs and turn over a new leaf, and began to seek the true knowledge of God

I want my sisters to stop prostituting and using men to get what they want instead become independent, respect themselves and live as true ladies should

No one will hate another human being because of the color of their skin or any ignorant reason at all

The entire universe will live off of love peace, joy, happiness, and more love

Young and Old male or female will not be afraid to walk through the streets

We won't have innocent children being shot, molested or killed

My community will began to rebuild the town for the better so that the it is safe, clean and a place to call home

Entertainers of all kind will watch and say what they do and keep in mind the children are watching and they look up to them

I myself will make peace with my enemies and those that I have hurt

I also will confess my sins to God and ask for his help and to please show me my purpose, lead me the right way

God will heal this world he will put an end to all negativity that is happening here on earth WHEN THE SUNRISES........

SECTION III:

HIGHER POWER

(JEHOVAH)

A cry for help (calling out to God)

The pressure to escape, crime, poverty and fear my life depends on it don't know where to go or who to turn to feeling alone like a dog without a home,

God you are the only one who can save me, tell me, show me where in life am I supposed to be help me get rid of these thoughts of worry I am losing focus reality is getting blurry I am afraid and don't know why,

God this anger, fear and shame take it away help me to grow and mature so I will not do foolish things can you hear me crying out to you why are you ignoring me please Father listen to me I need you,

Rescue me not only me but my peers are lost as well it's like we all drowning in sin please don't let the devil win you said to trust in you so I am giving my all to you teach us how to love let us surrender unto you and bring peace back into our mind and hearts so that it then will spread throughout the world.

Free us:

Lord my brothers and sisters are in trouble please free us from the power of sin,

Free us from satins wicked traps he is out to kill and destroy us,

Free us of drugs, violence, adultery, sex, diseases and negative thinking,

Get rid of the wickedness that weighs us down heal the world Lord,

Can you hear our cries will you rescue us from misery,

For the wrong things of this world my brothers and sisters lust,

We have misrepresented you we no longer rely and depend on you,

This is why problems have invaded the world,

Lord forgive us for the wrong things we are doing I have faith you will save us,

We are trapped in a world of confusion and hate,

Lord we need your help please help us now before it is too late

I ask you and will not stop asking you Lord from this destruction please free us.

God Is Good:

I am a witness that God is loving and forgiving,

Because of my Great wonderful God I am still alive,

Thank you for taking me out of so many negative situations,

God taught me how to love and treat people with respect,

Showed me how to be there for my family in the right way,

God changed my wrong steps to the right steps,

My message cannot be misunderstood,

I am a prime example that God is good.

I thank God for protecting me and not turning away from me

I thank him for letting me go through the trials and tribulations letting me see what is that I must do and I should live my life,

I thank God for blessing me with Knowledge, wisdom, and understanding and giving me the courage to help others and share his word with my brothers and sisters.

I thank God for making me strong when I was at my weakest point

I once caused harm on others walked in darkness but now that I have given my life to God I know he will be my everlasting light.

God took me away from evil people, places and things he washed away my sins God you are my true father, at times I cannot find the words to say it so I have many ways to praise you every day if it wasn't for you God I could have been left for dead in my hood but I stand here and can testify today that God Good.

I know God forgives:

I have sinned time after time over and over been beat down by my own mistakes and poor choices the guilt had me feeling ashamed and the shame got me feeling guilty it's like I am walking straight into death with my eyes wide open refusing to see the truth;

Suddenly I am placed in this cold cell and reality sets in the truth smacks me in the face now how I can see, I see that I put myself and a serious predicament my negative ways and irrational thinking have landed me here I can't blame anyone I did this so now I must face the consequences.

I began to think about what my parents and Grandparent taught me which is believe in God turn to him when life begins to get hard ask him for help show me the way to make it through as he renews me I can see and feel the change I am understanding and seeing things for what they really are so I ask God to keep me away from negative people places and things all I want to do is live a good life spend time with my family and love my beautiful wife and be the best father I can be to my daughter.

No more troubled times God is my protector I am thankful morning noon and night for his love guidance and discipline I will cherish each moment that I praise and thank him can anyone out there relate to how I feel if so you will know that God forgives and this is real.

Acknowledgements: recognizing those who have always showed me true love and support through the good and bad times and always kept it real with me I got nothing but love for you all

A MOTHER'S LOVE:

Sometimes I can't find the words to tell you how much I
care about you and love you and that our friendship means
the world to me it is priceless.

I also know that I haven't been the greatest son and I
apologize for any grief that I may have caused your sweet
tender heart.

One thing I know for sure is that I am thankful for having a
mother like you some one who is understanding, forgiving
and has a great sense of humor they say a man is nothing
without a good woman no I think different I feel a man is
nothing without a Good mother.

You have been here for me every step of the way wrong or
right you never left me in the dark you never condoned to
my wrong doing but always praised me for doing the right
things in life.

When I was sick with the chickenpox it was you who took
care of me, whenever I had a cold it was you who warmed
the soup made me tea and rubbed Vicks on my chest and
back and tucked me in the bed.

Even today you still love me the same your love never
changes it only gets stronger you are the role model that I
adore and I may not have all of your ways but there are a
few things I have picked up and that I ask GOD to bless me
with and that is your courage, wisdom, strength, patience,
loving heart, and humbleness.

When it comes to having that true friend in my life you are
the one I can always depend on through thick and thin
because of you I am starting to become even more
spiritually strong, mentally strong and physically strong
just the way you are.

You have shown me that hard work does pay off and to get
to the top you have to climb hard stay focused and if I fall
down get back up and start climbing again you have taught
me that it is better to be honest instead of dishonest.

To My Father:

I want to thank you for all the things that you have done for me although we have been through some rough times I want you to know I love you and always will. Thank you for blessing me with this talent of writing being able to express my thoughts and feelings with a pen and paper when it was hard to verbally express myself thank you for being my Father and friend and for teaching me all the good things that have brought me this far no longer do I look back at the past because it's exactly what it is the past no one is perfect we all make mistakes is what I am learning as a man let us just do our best to live life in the right way and continue to pray for God's love at all times again thank you Dad for being there for me.

For my Daughter Victoria and my Niece Payton:

It is important that you two love each other and be more than cousins be best friends always look out for one another and be kind to each other never fight with each other if you feel you are upset with each other walk away until you can calm down and then talk it out you two are the first Grand children in the family so it is important that you do good and be respectful yes always respect yourselves so that others will instantly know when you walk through the door that you are too be respected and remember the family loves you both and always will and we will be here to help you and guide you along the way with those tough choices that life sometimes dishes out to us we will do our best to protect you but there will be times that you both have to be strong enough and wise enough to protect each other I encourage you to do good in school get good grades and become successful Black women and remember my Daughter Victoria Daddy loves you and also My Niece Payton Uncle Pop loves you make us proud and no matter what always stand strong and define yourselves as Beautiful intelligent black women because you Represent all the Robinson women in the family.

MY LOVE: (AKEYA FAITH JENKINS)

When I think of you and all that we share
I find my self lifted high over the
World

The power of your love is unexplainable I never knew
Love could be so real and feel this good

If you were here with me right now I would turn the lights down low
Gently lay you on the bed kiss you all over your body nice and slow.

A vision of you and I making love in the rain travels through my mind
I will take you to paradise and keep you there forever bless your
Tender heart with constant pleasure
Adore you know matter how stormy the weather

You and I are like hand and glove lock and key
Water and tea I am for you, you are for me
Always you and I shall stay together.

Love always
Pop

P/s: Smile 4 me

Thank you:

I want to take the time to thank everyone who will and has already been supporting my writing encouraging me to express myself through pen and paper my journey has not been easy I have hit some bumps in the road but I am thankful that God keeps me lifted up and when things seem as if they are going wrong he provides a better way for me and he has blessed me with a Beautiful wife and Daughter a loving family my parents my brother my uncles and aunts and my friends my Harris ave crew you'll are the best and to those who will go out and buy my book and all the others to follow I want to say thank you and I appreciate the love and it is important that you know my words are for the world every race young and old there are things that I have been through and witnessed good and bad and this is my way of sharing it thins I write will make you laugh maybe shed a tear make you feel romantic and want to hug and kiss the one you love but whatever my words do to you just know that they are my words and they are real from my heart my last message would be to the world lets live in peace stop the killings there is violence all over the world and only we can stop the madness by showing love and respect I want to shout out my Home Freeport better known as the port Knox also shout out to Amityville Wyandanch Hempstead, Roosevelt, Harlem, Brooklyn , Bronx charlotte North Carolina and Atlanta Georgia just a few places I had to shout out love is love

Before I continue on doing what I do best

I want to take time out to THANK GOD for giving

Me the strength, wisdom, and courage to share my words

With my brothers and sisters all over the world.

My words are for everyone, all races!

I also want to thank my Mother and Father for always

Being in my corner through the Good and bad I love you both

Your love and guidance is truly appreciated.

To my brother who I love with all my heart its time

For us to be the men GOD has instructed us to be

When you cry I cry when you're happy I am happy

I love you always.

To my aunts and uncles I thank you for

Being there for me and always keeping it real with me especially

Through those times I was doing wrong you still continued to

show me love

To my Cousin and big sister Simone I love you girl just keep

The faith knows that God is good and I will always be here for

you.

This next shout out is very special I send this to my

Queen, yeah I 'm talking to you Grandma I love you

Stay strong for us God is watching over you.

To the rest of my cousins I love you all dearly and remember

God is good so pray and began to make those changes that

Are needed so that your life will be a lot more pleasant.

To my friends: Shem, Sean, Kwasi, Justine, Pdb Nation, Justice, Starmel, my boy George and I have to shout out the entire fade masters love is love

And I have the thank my brother in spirit my friend Jamel Harden who helped me and supported me to get this book done so that I can share my words with the world I thank you for encouraging me and taking the time out to help me.

KE KE:

IT WAS TRULY A PLEASURE MEETING YOU,
I ENJOYED DANCING WITH YOU
AND WATCHING YOUR BEAUTIFUL SMILE
LIGHT UP THE ROOM.

AS I WRITE THESE WORDS TO YOU I AM
SITTING HERE THINKING ABOUT YOUR BEAUTIFUL
EYES, SWEET LIPS, SEXY CHOCOLATE BROWN SKIN
IT'S NOT HARD TO TELL YOU HAVE THE
POWER TO HYPNOTIZE MANY MEN.

WHAT'S IT LIKE TO HOLD YOU IN MY ARMS,
RUN MY FINGERS THROUGH YOUR HAIR,
NIBBLE ON YOUR PRETTY LITTLE EAR AND
CARESS YOUR SOUL ARE THE THOUGHTS'
THAT'S GENERATING THROUGH MY MIND.

RIGHT NOW YOU ARE IN VIRGINIA SLEEPING LIKE
A INNOCENT BABY AND I M HERE IN New York
UNABLE TO STOP THINKING ABOUT YOU I KNOW
KIND OF CRAZY IS'NT IT.

YOU ARE A WOMAN TO BE RESPECTED NOT
NEGLECTED OR TREATED UNFAIR,
THE WAY YOU CROSS MY MIND,
DO YOU THINK OF ME THE SAME WAY
CAN YOU FIND A SPECIAL PLACE IN YOUR HEART
FOR ME AND LET ME LOVE YOU UNTIL THE END OF TIME.

MY LIFE: WHAT A JOURNEY IT'S BEEN

About Me

I am a poet writing of my pain or things that I may have witnessed the romance that I write about I guess you can say that's the gentle side of me and how I feel a woman should be treated.

I am a person living life one day at a time praying daily for mercy and forgiveness because my sins are many.

I am your son hiding my depression, shame, and guilt. I am a man who is trying his best to make a good impression and make many changes in his life for the better.

I am your friend even if you are not mine although some may feel that's not right it's fine with me.

I am a dreamer a wisher wishing that this whole world was peaceful and every race could live as one.

I am a man who has thought about suicide and tried but never was successful and I thank GOD I wasn't.

I was a child and a teenager who really can't complain because although there were rough days life was not all that.

Now I am a man still living and learning who has overcome many trials and tribulations.

I am thankful for my scars and hard head lessons because it reminds me not to make the same mistake twice.

I am the man sitting next to you asking you to care I am your best friend hoping that you'll be there when I need you.

Cannot understand:

Some cannot comprehend the life I live the trials and tribulations I have faced the time and effort I put into people who I thought was real but turned out to be a waste of time;

No one will ever understand my hardcore attitude unless they have walked the same path of being stabbed, incarcerated, suicidal, broke, hood rich tricked into feeding my heart to an evil unworthy woman;

It's all good because through all the madness and sadness many lessons were learned my mind is stronger and I owe it all to Almighty God so each day that he opens my eyes I thank him for the blessings he has given me.

I'm not afraid to lust, love hate, nor kill but I think it's better to keep negativity out of my life and at all times stay to myself and keep it real by staying sucker free and keep my ass out of jail.

What's the benefits of being a thug and cool about going to jail or being plunged in the ground six feet deep it doesn't add up can anyone tell me how it got like this black men and women lost in society blinded by all that is unreal.

This is why I keep my head high and never let no man or woman discourage me I am a black man and will be until the day I die, I am not the black man you will catch with a gun a knife or drugs but what you will get from me is education because my life is history.

I encourage my people to examining the fight you are in because more than likely you are fighting for the wrong cause keep your eyes open your minds fresh fill it with truth and knowledge because for ignorance wisdom is the cure

Doing my best to move on:

I am doing all I can to keep the past behind me, but at times it creeps up on a brother from out of nowhere like a nightmare from hell, guilty of sin yes I am who isn't though I know I am not the only one I have don't things I never wanted to do and fell victim to a lot of negativity due to situations I put myself in but that is for me to deal with I have and I will.

Where I am from we call it the hood but is it really the hood if it is it's because we have no respect for our community and we are the ones to blame for making it hood,

If we come together and build our community up just maybe it will be a better place for all of those who reside in the neighborhood.

Crack feigns, hustlers, pimps prostitutes and pushers are everywhere children being left alone all hours of the night does anybody care look at that sister over there she used to be so fine but now she is turning tricks battered and abused lost in a unrealistic world.

When I pray at night I ask God to let my brothers and sisters see the light before it is too late it's time to get right with God get right with your life a change must come and it must come right now God may your will be done.

We waste so much time and energy fighting amongst ourselves when we should be fighting for our children to have a better education and for our community to be drug and violent free but we are falling into society's trap so who is the joke on am I right or wrong.

We must take a stand and demand respect, unity, peace and love back into not only our community but in our minds and hearts I pray God teaches us how to love again how to live in peace and be positive productive individuals.

I am doing my best to move on but when I see my people still hurting caught up in the struggle it's hard to close my eyes to what's really going on but I have to be careful not to get caught up by going back in to lend a helping hand so I ask God for insight to do things right to help my brothers and sisters, and do my best to move on

Fighting with the Devil in my cell:

At night my thoughts run wild,

So many painful memories flood my brain,

I catch flashbacks of the wicked things I have done,

The streets really made me a cruel animal,

So much damage I've caused to a lot of lives,

Innocent and non-innocent,

God will you forgive me?

Locked in this cell,

Fighting with satin,

Trying so hard to maintain,

My body is burning with guilt and shame,

Somebody help me ,

I am losing myself,

I just want to close my eyes and sleep this pain away,
but I can't it hurts too bad,

The devil won't let me rest, it's like he is always trying to put me to the test even as I sit behind these dirty bars.

The gates are locked tight, not a place to hide nor run,

The gate won't crack until the morning,

God give me the strength to make it through the night without losing my mind,

Because being locked up in this cell is no joke, I'd rather have freedom and be broke than to have nightmares tossing and turning fighting with the Devil in my cell.

From the writer Donald Robinson To Whom It May Concern:

God's beautiful Creation you are but how long will it be before you open your eyes up to what's really going on how much longer will continue to fall victim to the evil that is seen and unseen but you know it's all evil.

Wasting time is all you are doing the streets are destroying you, you're respecting a bullshit code that no one respects the code you should be respecting and honoring is your children and the true family who loves you and only wants the best for you.

It seems like the only thing on your mind is a get rich quick money scheme and as usual you always defeat yourself never winning just losing, losing years out of your life because they are being spent behind bars and losing years with family because you're not with us but you expect us to have trust well that's hard to do.

How long will you continue to be ignorant are you dumb deaf and blind last time I checked you could function just perfectly fine the plan is to elevate not go down into the pit of hell with those who refuse to stand strong and do what is right.

I once thought how you think spoke how you talked but I realized I had to change I am on the outside looking in so I really don't expect you to see through the madness but I am here to tell you step back and take a look at what going down and maybe just maybe you will get hip to the game and begin to play to win like a true champion.

You so blinded by the negativity the fake and phony lifestyle you are not paying attention to the consequences that lie ahead of you so drink your last drink smoke that blunt until you get real high enjoy it until it's all gone because little do you know your freedom is about to be snatched away from you again, will you be able to handle it and stand strong because your family is tired of you getting into trouble than come crying for help but in the streets you the man mister big shot playing the devils game living in sin but now you reaching out for help and love I aint mad at you it's just why put yourself through this.

I hope you get wise and get the courage to change before it's too late remember you have children and family who love and need you the most important thing is being there for them enjoying the good times and consoling them through the bad times trust me you are needed by so many you just need to see it.

So just fall back from the wicked things you are involved in you won't get far I am not trying to offend you or anyone who reads this, but if it upsets you then I am doing my job and you realize your life must change so I hope these words shed some light on you and you check yourself from here on out get it together and stand strong like a black man is supposed to don't worry about what other people may have or what they may say about you run your own race in time you will be in the lead winning the race and the most unforgettable way so again don't be mad I am just speaking my mind with love from the writer Donald Robinson.

Respect it:

Please understand that I am only human I make bad choices and mistakes at times it does not mean I don't love, feel or hurt and it does not mean I am a bad guy either.

There are days that I am doing well and things come easy to me then there are those times shit just is not going right and want to spazz out and I might do so because I am doing my best to do the correct things in life and here comes a bump in the road that is really slowing me up whether it be people places or things it seems like it's always something.

All I want to do is be the best I can for God, my daughter wife and the rest of my true family and friends I say true because not everyone who claims they are family and friends will truly look out for my best interest some may even be thinking now he wrote this book I know he got money don't even know this is just another way for me to eat and make ends meet.

To those I have offended you will read it right here first hand I humbly apologize from my heart to yours I can only hope and pray you forgive me and accept it. If not at least I gave effort to make and mends and make things right between us especially if you ever caught me on one of those days I had too much to drink I definitely am sorry for whatever I said or done I know alcohol can bring out the worst in me at times.

I hope it's ok with you if I just keep it real because really I am simple man the only thing I want out of life as a husband and father is my wife and daughter to be happy and it's my duty to make sure they are happy as much as I can make them and a son to continue to put a smile on my parents face and make sure I am not worrying their hearts and as a brother to be the best big brother I can possibly be and the same goes for being a friend all I want is for my friends to accept me for who I am and never judge me because real friends don't do that.

Life is hard sometimes for a man out here no matter what race you are its just like that for some of us. I wasn't born with a silver spoon in my mouth I just eat with one, I can care less about those who threatened me and try to discourage me it just shows me how intimated of me you really are because truth be told I have always been in a class by myself you know on a whole different level so what others say and do is nothing to me I am keep on doing what I need to do to survive at all times.

Maybe the words I write will make me finally be heard and understood who knows only time will tell but either way my voice shall be heard I am a black man a leader in my own way and right so please don't bark up my tree you are surely starting the wrong kind of fight.

I got love for everyone never prejudice to known that's for fools those who plot on me I even will not hate you but I got my eyes on you all four of them (lol) I know you wish me pain suffering and death and even though I am a sinner I believe God knows my heart and he watches over me so I will never worry or fear no man.

And when that day comes when I am dead and gone or should I say until that day comes this is what you can expect from me, expect me to smile and be respectful lend a helping hand even if you don't want it but you know you need it. You might see me lose my call as I said I am not perfect and shit happens don't bother me I won't bother you love me and I will love you respect me and I will respect you more I am just a black man asking you to let me live my life and Respect it.

The Night I thought I wanted to Die:

Lights Flashing Eyes blinking why did I do it what was I thinking,

Family and friends people and general who heard about what I did now think different about me is crazy what's his problem yes I have problems and I don't know how to deal with the issues that are troubling my heart and I feel like I have no one to turn to I am not crazy my soul is hurting my heart is full of pain.

Mom and Dad are shouting is he going to live don't let my child die please save him I can hear Dad saying son what's wrong with you this is not the way but my body and mind is numb I hear nothing just let me die today.

My head is not straight the world is spinning around this pain it hurts so bad but suddenly I realize I don't want to die don't let my eyes close for good God keep them open let my heart continue to beat just take the pain away make me strong again I am sorry I was wrong the lights are flashing save me don't let me slip away into darkness I want to live I surrender to you a broken heart is all I have to give.

Three Times:

The 1st time the Lord gave me a sign,

But I was too stubborn to comprehend,

So I continued to ignore his message and proceeded to indulge in wickedness,

Travel with evil men and live an unclean life.

The 2nd time the Lord came to me and said, why are you not listening to me?

Why are you pretending to be someone you are not

He said to be do not be foolish do not do the devils dirty work,

He continued to say, my son Heaven is very loving and peaceful but the pit of hell is miserable and painful,

But still I refused to recognize the truth.

The 3rd time the Lord presented himself to me again he said to me please put away the bad things that you are doing let me show you a better way tired of the madness that I was going through I decided to give the Lord my attention because deep down inside I knew I needed help, correction, discipline and love and I knew I could not get it from the streets. But I had a question to ask? I said Lord whey do you want to lend your hand to a man who is full of sin? The Lord smiled, told me to come back home and as I grabbed hold of his hand and follow behind him I heard him say, I love you as my father does, and eternally I am your friend.

Until you touch down:

Painful Secrets are hidden within his heart,

Angry and confused trying to wash away the pain with drugs, alcohol and sex but still the problems remain to be the same.

Nightmares constantly haunting him blaming himself for what happened to his friend because he feels like it should be him locked in that cell,

Why did he let him take the gun is all he can ask himself was it meant to be this way my friend back in the belly of the beast no it's not supposed to be like this you should be out here in the world with your family and friends is this all the bullshit catching up to us because of past sins.

Looking forward to better days to spend with you again,

Waiting for my friend to be free praying for you and your loved one's daily and when you get home we have to play it by the book do things right fall back and push a legal gig 9-5 and enjoy life the right way but until you come home I am going to stand strong and hold you down love is love my friend.

Respect: Is What All God's Children Deserve no matter what color one may be

A FRIEND THAT CARES:

To see you under these circumstances brings pain to my
heart;
I never thought that you would be in my corner the way
you were;
I watched how your gentle eyes fought back tears when I
came into the visiting room I know I never wanted for us to
have a visit from jail.

I guess mama was right the eyes and heart never lie;
Because you are a friend that cares and I thank you for your
love and support you made my days and nights easier being
locked up waiting to be set free.

We have known each other for so many years but I didn't
think we would have the friendship that we do I know
sometimes we can really go at it but the truth it I love you
and I am honored you are my friend.

I felt so foolish to have you see me like this dressed in an
orange jumpsuit I am sorry I didn't tell you what I was
involved in but I really did not know how and I was scared
of losing your friendship.

You will always have a place in my heart no matter where I
may be I think about you and all my fears go away because
I know that I can count on you in the time of need because
you are a friend who cares...

Bad Name:

So young and immature she thinks having sex at an early age is cool but how wrong she is but she will soon find out the hard way that she was wrong,

The young boy down the block just a little older than her he got mad game she is slow to the jive he is talking so she falls for it and now he got her caught up,

She believes that he loves her because he is doing everything right flowers and candy a movie and dinner here and there but now he moves in on her and she gives him what he wants now he got it and he's gone,

Feeling ashamed and played she realizes she was wrong but the thing is now homeboy is telling his friends how easy she gave up the ass giving her a bad name and when she denies other guys they slander her name even worse,

Ladies this is a serious thing so before you give away you precious body to a man please hopefully you will be smart and do it the Godly way and wait until you're married.

You must understand that your body is a special temple that God has blessed you with so don't ruin it for anyone be smart and don't rush into having sex you have plenty of time for that focus on education and becoming successful.

BLACK BUTTER FLY:

To my Black Sister so strong and beautiful I want you to
know that you are and always will be appreciated because
there are men out here who respect you and for all that you
stand for I see how hard you work that job plus go to
school and take care of your family keep doing what you
do don't let no ignorant man pull you down don't let any
negative thing change your path stay positive.

Sometimes you are going to fall its ok just get up give it to
GOD and keep running your race no one said you had to
speed go at your own pace so that an the end you will have
achieved your goals fulfilled your purpose in life and never
feel unworthy.

I am here to tell you my BLACK BUTTER FLY trust in
GOD and life won't treat you unfair or seem so hard
remember that GOD sacrificed his only begotten son for
you so it is true he loves you and will not forsake you just
call on him and he will answer you.

Have faith and pray all the time as much as you can so
when those rough days come you will have enough strength
to fight and win instead of falling down submitting to sin I
don't care if you want to hit the wall, kick the car, scream
and curse just don't throw in the towel and don't let
ignorance get the best of you.

Be free and spread your wings like an eagle lift your voice
up so that every one hears you and knows who you are
show every man that you are to be respected never
neglected because you are a strong BLACK BUTTER
FLY.

IF YOU TRULY SEE YOURSELF AS A MAN
TREAT OTHERS WITH RESPECT, BE MAN ENOUGH
TO KEEP THE PEACE,   SAVE A LIFE
DON'T TAKE ONE.

TO KILL ANOTHER HUMAN BEING JUST TO GET A
REPUTATION IS NOT COOL IT IS PURE IGNORANCE!

IF YOU CAN DO THAT I SAY THAT IS GANGSTA!

Do you think you are tough because you carry a gun
or you shot someone only to end up in prison or
spending your life on the run I really don't see what's
so gangster about that?

My message to the youth and the older brothers and
female too who are violent, learn to be nonviolent a
person's life is to be valued and respected there is a
solution for every problem it does not make you a
coward to handle things the right way or walk away
with your head up high knowing you did the right
thing just think if more people would handle
problems wisely it would eliminate a lot of wrongful
deaths and brothers and sisters going to prison.

MR. POLICE OFFICER:

The man in the BMW was speeding but you let him continue on I am not going to say what race he was or who was right and wrong but I wasn't speeding so why you pulling me over giving me a ticket.

I was standing on the corner waiting for the bus but you rolled up on me threw me on the ground and asked me where's the gun and drugs now you know that isn't right at all why do some of you cops have to be so fowl making the cool ones look bad what you don't understand is you're a man like me its ok for you to mistake me for a gangster, drug dealer or thief so I guess its ok for me to look at you as another crooked pig but that would make me ignorant just like you and that's not right either.

Don't think because you wear a badge and carry a gun that you can just treat people any kind of way you want this is why today women are scared when you pull them over or young teenagers panic when you come driving through they don't know if your going to shoot them or plant some crack on them. Why can't you just do your job the right way?

Your job is to protect and serve so please do so I understand your job is not easy and your just as afraid as we are but some where we have to come to an understanding and push for a change because as I said at the end of the day when you go home and take off that badge and gun you're a regular hard working man just as I am.

Questions and Thoughts:

What will become of him has he learned his lesson?
Does he realize that living behind bars is not a pleasant environment?
Or has he become accustomed to the jail house mentality.

What is your reality?
Doing Gods will is my reality living life in a healthy way Spiritually,
Mentally as well as physically.

How do you want to be treated?
I want to be treated as a human being not an animal, I don't want to be
looked down on because of my troubles in the past because no man or
woman is perfect every one has trials and tribulations in their lives at
one point or another.

Life is hard as we all know but its even harder once you have become
part of the system its like the world just got colder but even though
that's when we must take a deep breath and get stronger and as long as
we keep pushing giving constant effort believe me when I tell you the
sun will shine brighter and brighter each day.

So will he give up and return to the land of fools, or will he continue to
do the right thing no matter how hard things in life may seem or
become to be.

I think he's going to be just fine.

Never give up because only losers quit
If you started out on the right path stay on it
And if your not traveling on the right path I suggest you jump on it.

The right path is the joyful peaceful loving eternal living path.
But the wrong path is the path of Destruction and Death

Stop being selfish it's not all about you:

Once a again your family is sadden by the fact you are back in prison filled with much sorrow no bail because of the parole hold never thought they would have to relive this nightmare again it's not fair what you are doing to yourself as well as your family sure wish you could see the damage you are causing.

Brother your back behind that prison wall and those who love you are truly hurt please understand we love you and just want you to do better with your life when you are locked up so are we maybe not in the physical form but mentally we are.

It's time for you to think about finding a better way to live take care of your children and be the man you are supposed to be think about your children you are missing so much time with them before you know it they will be grown if you continue to make a life out of going back and forth to jail and how do you expect to have a relationship with them or even respect you.

You are burning bridges faster than you think I know you don't want to be there I can see it all in your face so I took the time out to pray for you and ask god to help you see reality for what it is and to please understand what you are doing hurts the ones who love you so please stop being selfish because it's not all about you

STOP LEAVING YOUR WOMAN ALONE:

Know matter what you do or the trouble you cause your woman always seems to stand by you. You're a dead beat dad a broke ass chump don't know the first thing about how to treat a lady but still she is by your side.

You are out in the streets sleeping with other females doing you not giving any thought about how you are hurting that beautiful woman you so call love you know the mother of your children who you step on day after day with your drug dealing, gambling, cheating and lies.

Oh shit but look what's good now you got your black ass locked up now you need her to hold your no good ass down you're nothing but a fucking clown. It's funny how you never thought about her while you were in the streets making a mess of your life hers and your children now you want to be a husband you should have been doing that while you were out in the world.

Look at you stressing why she is not home all insecure cursing her out on visits you a damn fool you the one who needs the visits and any way ass hole she's been working extra hours plus a second job because you left her out in the world fucked up so relax be easy and do your time concentrate on correcting your spirit, mind and heart so you don't repeat the same mistake again.

I tell my Black brothers your women need you out in the world not locked down behind bars because its not easy for them to handle things alone all of the time especially when you have a mort gauge to pay provide food, clothing and an education for the children so before you start flipping on your lady take a step back and check your self and stop leaving your woman out their in the world alone because a real man is just waiting to take your queen away from you.

ROMANCE: THE WILD AND HUMBLE LOVER IN ME

AFTER TONIGHT:

WHEN I LAY THE FOUNDATION OF LOVE
DOWN ON YOUR SOUL;
YOUR BODY WILL GO INTO CONFESSION
BECAUSE YOU CAN'T HANDLE THIS LOVE LESSON
I AM ABOUT TO GIVE YOU ITS JUST TOO POWERFUL.
TRUST ME MA, YOU WON'T KNOW WHAT TO
DO ONCE I'M DONE I GAURENNTEE
YOU HAVE NEVER ENCOUNTERED THIS TYPE OF ACTION.

AFTER TONIGHT, TOMORROW YOU WILL BE ON
THE PHONE WITH YOU FRIEND LIKE GIRL DADDY HIT ME
UP RIGHT,
HE SO GOOD HE GIVE A BLIND WOMAN BACK HER SIGHT
MAKE A SINNING LADY REPENT AND SCREAM SHE SEES THE
LIGHT.

I SEE SHORTY OVER THERE LISTENING TO MY WORDS
WITH HER LEGS WET CROSSED TIGHT
ITS COOL NO NEED TO FIGHT THE HEAVENLY FEELING
RELAX AND LET MY TONGUE GIVE YOU SOME SEXUAL
HEALING.

AFTER TONIGHT YOU WILL KNOW THAT PUSSY BELONGS TO
ME, JUST TELL ME WE'RE AND I'LL PUT MY DICK WE'RE
EVER YOU WANT IT TO BE.
EVERY TIME I SLIDE UP IN YOU THE WAY YOU SCREAM
MY NAME DRIVES ME INSANE.

AFTER TONIGHT YOU WILL TRULY KNOW WHAT MAKING
LOVE IS ALL ABOUT
YEAH I KNOW YOU OPEN OFF OF THE WAY I
BE EATING YOU OUT,
COME ON MA YOU DEALING WITH A PRO
THE ONE WHO MAKES YOUR BODY GLOW EVERY TIME
YOU FEEL MY FLOW.

BLACK RAIN:

I just wanted you to know

If you take your love from me my heart would be in pain,

I'm so deep in love with you I am not ashamed to admit it to the world let it be known,

Listen to how the music is softly playing as the ocean breeze soothes our bodies feel the love circulate through the room my soul yearns for you my heart burns for you beautiful woman I adore you,

Tonight I plan to find your hidden treasure I am going to inject your body with so much pleasure and I promise you I will not stop until I make your precious diamond shine,

Lay your head upon my chest let out bodies softly touch each other how beautiful it is to feel our hearts beat my hands begin to gently wander across your thighs as my tongue slowly converse with your breast,

Making love to you tonight is my only request it's a must that I practice what I preach and show you that I am your one and only no need to look any further after I put it down on you, you will know that I am the best,

The things you do to me drives me insane I am going to love you in so many ways all I want is to feel you shower me with your sweet black rain.

CHOCOLATE COVERED STRAWBERRIES AND CHERRIES: PT 1

Oh yeah it's me the irresistible poem writer, the one who's got you so suspicious because you heard through the grapevine that I am so nutritious and that I am the man who will give your body constant pleasure by all means.

So being that you're curious I figured you and I could dedicate ourselves to a night of chocolate covered strawberries and cherries to enhance your dreams.

At least when your thoughts are on me, so listen to my sexual plan

Lay back and relax this free of charge no tax with the 69 position included, let me melt into your body like hot wax; push this love affair to the max. Chocolate covered strawberries and cherries are a passion that's sweet I'm delighted and you're invited to a treat because I'm hot as fire ready to erupt like a volcano and let my lava flow all over your body you are my treat I am yearning for you like a dog in heat.

Chocolate covered breast I confess you are the best as you place your tender caramel nipples in my mouth, hands slowly caressing those beautiful thighs, check how I flip it on you and take a trip down south. Intoxicated off the heavenly sensation leading you to penetration goy you screaming give it to me daddy and I am not going to stop until I feel your body tremble and get weak my love is so good it's guaranteed to make you joyfully cry.

Tonight there will be no love making just strictly fucking I'm talking about that back breaking, head board hitting, bed shaking, grabbing the sheets, biting the pillow, pony tail pulling ass slapping type of fucking the kind of love or should I say freaky sex that will leave you curled up sucking your thumb ass if you were a new born baby.

Mixing this chocolate with your cream is better than any vanilla sundae supreme you know the kind of flavor that is every real man's dream. So this is why I have to take it to the extreme, open your legs and feel me dive in between your about to witness something never heard of or seen damn shorty your pussy got me hooked like a Fein.

Surrounded by strawberries and cherries no questions asked only sessions of exotic hot sex contemplating on what I am about to do next, rich thick chocolate dripping off of you tasting so good my sexy freak don't get it misunderstood because this love affair feels so good. And I'm feeling the way you work that cherry with your lips as you pour that creamy chocolate on my dick catching with your tongue before it touches my balls tongue so dangerous got me bouncing off the walls.

Feeling the way you greet my dick with great pleasure so it's only right I give it to you in every measure feel loves pressure as I push deeper to find your beautiful treasure after tonight you will have become my diamond for an eternity, and I am not going to surrender until daddy hears his little mommy screams she sees the light and feels the truth of love runs through your innocent veins yeah its going down like that.

Putting this love affair on delay would only cause me a valuable price to pay so act like you know and have it your way. I got a milk shake for you that's better than your favorite ice cream the protein I have for you is necessary the kind that will keep you warm all through the month of February I'm going to smoke you like some good old purple haze lick your body up and down get you soak and wet leave you in a daze bless your temple with an ultimate spark and blaze.

Pushing deeper inside you moving faster and faster like a run away money train my love flows through your body like the blood in your veins you got me open truly hypnotized off the doggy style position as I slide my dick into your round soft juicy ass moving with a slow motion giving you my magic potion enjoying the feeling of exotic sex being shared between you and I never losing concentration nor hesitating on causing you to reach your peak make your delicious body shout for joy legs over your head as we continue to tear up the bed.

I am sure to have you saying he's a hell of guy for real no lie, CHOCOLATE COVERED STRAWBERRIES AND CHERRIES is only for you and I so amateurs please no need to try, CHOCOLATE COVERED STRAWBERRES AND CHERRIES spread all over you boo this is what real experienced lovers do, remember always I love you.

COUNTLESS TIMES:

THROUGH COUNTLESS TIMES I
WILL LOVE YOU LIKE NO OTHER MAN CAN;

THROUGH COUNTLESS TIMES I WILL WORK
MY FINGERS TO THE BONE FOR YOU, GIVE
YOU WHATEVER YOU WAN'T AND NEED.

THROUGH COUNTLESS TIMES I PROMISE TO
CHERISH AND RESPECT YOU;

THROUGH COUNTLESS TIMES I WILL NEVER
STOP BEING YOUR FRIEND;

THROUGH COUNTLESS TIMES I WAN'T YOU TO KNOW
THAT I AM NOT IN THIS RELATIONSHIP FOR NOTHING,

THROUGH COUNTLESS TIMES YOU AND I ARE FOREVER
ONLY GOD HIMSELF CAN SEPARATE US NO ONE ELSE;

THROUGH COUNTLESS TIMES I'LL DO WHATEVER I
HAVE TO MAKE YOU SMILE;

THROUGH COUNTLESS TIMES I WILL HOLD YOU IN MY
ARMS NEVER LET GO AND SPOIL WITH LOVE AND KISSES;

THROUGH COUNTLESS TIMES I PROMISE NEVER
TO LEAVE YOU LONELY OR TURN MY BACK ON YOU
FOR ANY REASON;

THROUGH COUNTLESS TIMES YOU ARE MORE THAN I COULD
EVER WAN'T OR NEED I KNOW GOD HAS TRULY BLESSED ME
SO THROUGH COUNTLESS TIMES I WILL FULL FILL ALL OF
YOUR DREAMS AND SATISFY YOU MIND BODY AND SOUL
THROUGH COUNTLESS TIMES.

EMPTY WITHOUT YOU:

I feel it's time you and I sit down, talk and work things out.
 These problems you and I are experiencing just don't make sense
And honestly I can't read your mind I need to know how you feel
Because right now our love does not seem real.

You and I share the same life not to mention the same bed
 So tell me why do I feel empty without you, let's bring the sunshine
Back into our lives be happy like other husbands and wives, there is
No need for our hearts to carry around so much pain.

All we have to do is communicate, baby if we don't it's only
Going to cause us to separate so why not be mature do this the right
Way get our relationship straight continue this love like it was our
First date.

Girl the way you put it on me is unexplainable to me it's something
That no other woman could ever do, you are a special part of me
Through good and bad for richer or poor you I will always adore.

For my wife:

Our life together the love you and I share is no fairytale,

It was meant to be joined together by the power of God,

No man or woman can ever separate us nor break our trust,

When I met you I knew I could not let you just pass me by,

I was hypnotized off your beautiful soft chocolate brown skin,

Deep in your love is where I always want to be,

You are my queen my best friend and I are never going to let you go,

Having you in my life is such a pleasure,

I am always looking forward to returning home to spend time with you,

I just want to hold you in my arms, and run my fingers through your hair,

It might sound crazy but every minute spent with you is a precious moment,

My heart skips a beat as we float on air making love,

Staring into each other's eyes never wanting this moment to disappear,

I want to be locked away on love land with you pleasing you for an eternity,

You are the lock and I am the key that gets you open always and forever you are my Angel I love you.

GIVE IT TO ME:

Her body feels so good,

My chest gently presses against her soft breast,

I just want to touch and kiss her everywhere,

Physically I am going to show her how much I care,

I am going to take here exactly where she is supposed to be as I look into her beautiful I eyes I whisper don't be afraid your love is al l I want and need so please give it to me.

I am on top of her she is on top me she lets me know just what she wants my tongue to do and where it should be the love lessons we are sharing is mind blowing,

The more she frees herself and unwind I can tell that she wants to be pleased all kind of ways and she doesn't want this moment to be interrupted because she is her groove showing me how she gives it up in the bedroom and I have to be honest mama is experienced.

We must make this night last forever or until both of our bodies give in there's nothing wrong with lovers getting freaky get the whip cream and handcuffs the bunny ears and earmuffs lol or how about making love in the rain better yet a pool of strawberries and ice cream rub some ice down your back in between the crack of your ass relax and let me fulfill your dream push my shaft and your sweet stream I promise to move slow and be gentle oh baby please give it to me.

Those eyes are so sexy and peaceful I can't explain what your love does to me so many feeling I have inside can I share them all with you until the sun comes up can you feel the sex in the midnight air tonight will be an exciting event you say your love is all mine so baby please give it to me.

HUNTING FOR LOVE

LOVE WHY HAVE YOU GONE AWAY,
YOU ALWAYS GAVE ME YOUR WORD YOU'DE NEVER
LEAVE,
NOW LIKE A LONELY LOST BIRD I SEARCH FOR LOVE
TELL ME WE'RE DID YOU GO.

WHAT DID I DO WRONG,
WAS IT SOMETHING I SAID
I'M LOOKING FOR ANSWERS BECAUSE I DON'T
UNDERSTAND,
ALL I KNOW IS THAT I SPEND MANY TEAR FULL NIGHTS
IN OUR EMPTY BED.

SOME SAY LOVE COMES LOVE GOES
I GUESS ITS TRUE BECAUSE LOVED GOT STRIPPED
AWAY FROM ME FASTER THAN A HOOKER TAKES OFF
HER CLOTHES.

LOVE YOU CAN MAKE ONE FEEL SO GOOD
BUT THEN YOU CAN ALSO MAKE A PERSON FEEL A
GREAT DEAL OF PAIN.

STILL DAY AFTER DAY I PRAY YOU RETURN TO ME
WHAT EVER IT TAKES TO GET LOVE BACK IN MY LIFE I
WILL DO LOVE WE'RE ARE YOU I NEED YOU PLEASE
COME RESCUE ME, LOVE, LOVE, LOVE.

HYNOTIZED:

Fascinated by her love she has me captivated, she relaxes my mind body and spirit making her smile and creating a beautiful life with her is truly all my pleasure my heart skips a beat as I look into her gentle eyes damn this woman got me Hypnotized.

The affection she gives to me is like no other Joy is all I want to give to her in return I appreciate her wisdom and strength the respect she has for herself is so amazing God has definitely blessed me because a woman like her is once in a life time so it's only right I make her mine damn look at that sexy walk cant take my eyes off of her I must be Hypnotized.

Without you in my life where would I be, lost weak in the knees promise you will always be by my side be my light when my days become dark you know how your love shines upon my world the heart never lies the night I met you I knew you were my everlasting Grand prize Damn you seem to have me Hypnotized.

The romanced and intimate bond you and I share is incredible, your kisses soft sweet and delicious pleases my soul always enjoying every moment of mentally and physically loving one another playing in your hair nibbling on your ear caressing your tender chocolate thighs got me so Hypnotized.

I'm Getting in that

Looking at the body on you got me like Damn I want to know how you feel you look so good and I know I would look good and feel good in you as well.

As I get close to you your scent hits my nose damn you smell good and the way you wearing that leather got me just wanted to feel you.

Can I get a test ride I want to know how you ride hit them corners slam on the brakes and slide.

I'm amazed by the firm grip I'm doing my best to rip it but your body is so strong I see you staying in control cause losing control would be dangerous for both of us but you start to swerve a little so I catch you I got it under control I'm not going to let us crash I am enjoying the ride you are giving me

This test ride was the best ever I know now I want to have you on a daily basis show you off so someone needs to get the sales men and let him know I want this Red BMW right here because I am getting in that.

I JUST WANTED TO TELL YOU:

Definitely you are the one I desire to be with forever
But something is holding us back stopping us from
enjoying that genuine pleasure

Is it me is it you? Only if I knew what to do
Because the woman I want in my life is you
Everything about you is incredible
Everything about you is beautiful

Day and night my heart burns to be next to yours
This love I am giving away surely belongs to you
And it seems like I am letting my only true friend and
love slip away

I guess I just want you to know that no matter what
happens you are and always will be that special
someone I love until my last day.

I want to be next to you:

I don't want to do anything except to be next to you;

There's nothing better than holding you in my arms expressing my affection to you but this distance between us is killing me all I want to do is to be next to you.

So many hot sunny days are going by without us being together I miss the late night walks through the park, or along the beach around town just you and I in love I truly miss those moments I just want to be next to you.

I need to be there with you but instead I am here locked in this cell dressed in orange tears drop from my eyes thinking of you all I want to do is to be next to you.

I cannot change what has happened or the bad times we experienced but I can make our future beautiful, warm and pleasing I vow to love you better than ever because all I want to do is to be next to you.

I WANT TO KNOW:

I WANT TO KNOW HOW YOUR LIPS TASTE;
BECAUSE I GOT A JONES IN MY BONES FOR YOU,

I WANT TO KNOW HOW POWAERFUL YOUR LOVE IS;
I'M FEELING YOU ARE YOU FEELING ME;

I WANT TO KNOW WHAT IT FEELS LIKE TO
HEAR YOU SCREAM MY NAME;
I WANT TO KNOW WHAT MAKES YOU SMILE
AND PLEASES YOUR HEART.

I WANT TO KNOW EVERYTHING ABOUT YOU
YOU'RE PAST, FUTURE, GOOD AND BAD;

I WANT TO KNOW WHAT WILL IT TAKE TO MAKE YOU
MINE
CAN WE DISCUSS THIS OVER CANDLE LIGHT
DINNER AND WINE
JUST TELL ME WHAT TIME

BECAUSE I REALLY WANT TO KNOW.

LAST NIGHT I HEARD YOU CRY:

I could not sleep at all last night I wish we could have talked before
they came and took me away,
I regret the silly fight we had I didn't have a chance to apologize,
I was not even able to say good bye now I lay in this cold cell
tossing and turning fighting hard to shut this nightmare out of my
mind but every time I close my eyes I can hear you cry.

You are out there alone in that big world,
I am alone in this big prison full of stress praying to GOD
None of these clowns try to put my knuckle game to the test because
it's going to be real painful for who ever I bump heads with.

You come to visit me with pain and tears in your lonely eyes
I try not to notice but how can I avoid your pain, I talk to you on the
phone we laugh and joke but its not the same and when the operator
clicks on and says you have 60 seconds your voice drops so low and
sad they lock me in I try to sleep but every time I close my eyes I can
hear you cry.

So much sorrow my foolish ways and fast life style has temporarily
damaged us damn when I get out of this cage I have to do right be a
man and work a 9-5 and make up the lost time between us. I am
sorry I caused your heart a great deal of pain I visualize us kissing
and holding hands I want to sleep but I can't because every time I
close my eyes I can hear you cry.

When I Close My Eyes

I visualize you wearing a stimulating gown, skin soft and light brown.
Beautiful long jet black hair dropping below your slender waist, smile exquisite
As a rainbow. You and I pleasantly walk hand in hand along the shore while
Love takes us on a romantic journey.

Holding you in my arms, our hearts begin to silently speak, your kiss soothes,
Me like the morning breeze, the fragrance of your sexy tender body pleases my
As your eyes glisten with life causing my love for you to naturally over flow.

 Your lips delicately kiss my neck; the shadow of your love warms my soul,
While resting my head upon your breast, joy is what I feel when you and I are
Together baby girl you are true meaning of peace.

I promise to never harm you nor interrupt the everlasting bond you and I share
Because it's not easy finding a woman who's honest, understanding, fair and
Wise I just want you to know this is how I feel and what I see when I close my
Eyes.

DDR 2

My plan is to love you the best way I possibly can, these feelings I have for you are the truth I just want you to trust in me and let my love set you free this is not a game I have no time to pretend.

I can careless about your past what happen with those other guys, you're my Lady now and I am going to treat you like a Queen I 'm going to show you what romance is all about.

I want to be your lover and eternal friend let me see you smile you know how that warms my soul. I write these words also in my heart you and I will always be together never apart just you and I taking on the world you know how much I love you girl.

Lay in my arms feel me relax your mind and body, get attached and lose control pleasing you is my goal without a doubt I am convinced you are for me and I am for you.

Soft chocolate brown skin beautiful from head to toe making love to you nice and slow bodies' hot and wet sex so good you'll never forget how I make your body glow.

I will accomplish what no man has yet done take you places you've never gone sexually. I'm going to heal your heart because I know it's been scorned just take my hand let me lead the way as I bring you into a new day.

SECRET GARDEN:

Take my hand and let me lead you to paradise, there we will elaborate and manifest our love to its highest degree fall into a trance and let romance set us free.

Total gratification is what you will feel, sexy lady you are a special part of me. You are my dream come true, you have my heart, honor and respect in more ways than one; day and night I seek to hold and comfort you.

I'm hypnotized by your sweet kiss and the fragrance of your hair, all that you stand for is I truly cherish. You often ask me how long do I plan to love you well honestly you can stop asking because I am not going any where I'm going to love you whether I am alive or dead.

True love can never be denied or stopped, life without you is meaning less my entire world, dreams and goals I want to share with you and only with you.

My beautiful princess you may control the lock but I regulate the key, and right now I am looking into your eyes yearning to get you open. I can hear our bodies silently speak to one another as the wind touches us with a gentle breeze.

The moon and stars light the sky your tender affection feels so good it's making me joyfully cry can't you tell by the twinkle in my eye, as I plant my seed of love into your secret garden.

Tonight I am going to be your love maestro,
The way my fingers will play with your body is
Guaranteed to excite you watch how I tease you
As I softly bite you.

I am going to make love to you with perfection
Check how I initiate this romance as I began to examine
That beautiful treasure inside your pants.

You're beauty has got my full attention, body posture
Showing off the sexiest attitude as you began to free your
Self and get nude.

Feel my lips flirt with your breast while I work my
Way down to the middle given you my ultimate test
Unwrapping your legs with my tongue causing you to
Get hot and wet.

I can tell by the look in your eyes that I got you
Hypnotized, you want to know why and how I got you
Feeling this way, sorry ma it's an ancient black man
Secrete.

Your gentle touch has an unbelievable influence over me
The way your lips captivate my soul really makes a
Brother loses control.

The warmth of your breast soothes my chest as I
Slowly push my pipe deep inside your mainline giving
You every drop of my manpower as I flip it on you and
Hit it from behind until the final hour.

you know how you, Like it rough because you think your
tough but I got news ,For you shorty I'm not going to
stop until you scream pop that's enough

UNDRESSING YOU WITH MY EYE:

Eyes locked on your body as if I had ex ray vision
thinking of ways I can please your precious temple;

As you let your hair down slowly my lips began to
massage your tender neck holding you in my arms lost in
paradise wow this feels really nice.

Hands rubbing you up and down unbuttoning your blouse
unstrapping your Victoria secrete braw taking off your
skirt causing both our body temperatures to rise you want
me I can see it in your eyes.

My mission is almost complete let's not forget those sexy
red panties oh I'm sorry I mean that sexy red thong.
Damn girl I hope you're prepared for some real sexual
action and satisfaction now off comes the thong look at
you laying on the bed so delicious and sweet open up
your legs and let daddy eat.

UNSTOPPABLE

IN FRON'T OF THE FIRE PLACE,
LICKING YOU UP AND DOWN;
INTOXICATED OFF OF YOUR SWEET TASTE
ENJOYING THE SATISFYING LOOK THAT 'S
WRITTEN ALL OVER YOUR BEAUTIFUL FACE.

HANDS CARESSING YOUR TENDER CHOCOLATE BROWN
SKIN,
BODY FEELING SO GOOD AS I BEGAN TO DEEPLY PUSH IN,
GOT ME FLIPPING LIKE A MASTER FROM SHAOLIN.

MAKING OUR WAY TO THE LIVING ROOM COUCH
LEGS HIGH UP IN THE AIR,
LIPS NIBBLING ON YOUR EAR,
PULLING ON THAT LONG BLAACK GORGEOUS HAIR
UNLOCKING MY TREASURE
GIVING YOU ETERNAL PLEASURE.

OUT ON THE BALCANI MAKING LOVE IN THE RAIN
SLAPPIN THAT ASS PUSHING HARDER AND HARDER
YOU FREAK FASCINATED WITH PAIN
SUCKING ALL OVER YOUR BODY LIKE A CANDY CAIN;

YOU AND I BRING A NEW MEANING TO THE WORD SEX
THE WAY YOU AND I MAKE LOVE IS
EXCITING, UNCONTROLLABLE, INCREDIBLE, UNFORGETTABLE
CRAZY INSANE UNSTOPPABLE.

WHEN EVER FOR EVER:

I Love you when ever… For Ever There was so much I wanted to say and so much you needed to say. Many conversations between us within the ether. So much love we share When Ever For Ever…

Knowing that I love you & you love me, knowing that I miss you and you miss me. Whether you and I are far apart or close together When Ever…For ever… Whether times are good or bad, When Ever… For Ever… Knowing that when you hurt I hurt, knowing that I will always be here for you & you will be here for me

WHEN EVER… FOR EVER…

Knowing that I care for you with all my heart & you care for me with all your heart, understanding that our friendship could never be broken because what you and I share is priceless. WHEN EVER… FOR EVER…

Knowing that I understand you and you understand me, no matter how much we try to hide our emotions or feelings the small details tell me when you are happy or sad WHEN EVER… FOR EVER…

Knowing that you will always be my Queen and I am your King regardless the tides are rough or smooth, WHEN EVER…FOR EVER… Knowing that I have given you strength and you have given me strength to make our days easier to deal with. Trusting that you and I will always be faithful and loyal to one another, feeding each others hearts the unconditional love we need and deserve, WHEN EVER … FOR EVER…

WHEN LOVE IS GONE:

Tears fall
Moods change
Life seems so strange
I feel like I don't belong
When love is gone

I can't eat or sleep
I just want to be left alone
Don't feel like hanging out with the boys
I'm trying to figure out were I went wrong
Because love is gone

I want her back so bad but I know it's too late
Thought she was my soul mate
I made a big mistake
Now another man has her heart
My whole world just fell apart

Memories of her beautiful smile is all I have
My love for will always remain strong
This is my sad song
This is what happens to a man
When love is gone

Street life and Violence

DO YOU HEAR ME CRYING?

Trapped in a world of darkness living a cold blooded life every where I go I have to carry a gun or a knife;

I can't even enjoy a pleasant day with my son or my wife because I am too stressed about what possibly could happen to them if one of my enemies catches me sleeping;

This is how it is when your playing that dirty game of money, drugs and murder damn you just don't know how bad I want my life back how I would give any thing to be me to just work a 9-5 and not have to worry about am I going to die or go to jail today;

Night and day I pray for a peaceful life because the devil is on my ass I'm trying to get away from him but he just to strong, what am I doing wrong something is missing;

Theirs just got to be a better way if I make it home to wake up in the morning that means I lived to see another day Please LORD show the right way to live, my sins are many and so heavy Please take them away give me a second chance because I have too much to live for.

No more negativity I just want eternal happiness can I enjoy days nights months and years with my family without them worrying about me and shedding tears on the outside I may be smiling but on the inside I am slowly dieing GOD do you hear me crying…

DRUG MONEY:

I got rich off of drug money;
I got power off of drug money;
I was able to buy houses, cars, clothes, jewelry even the
police with my drug money.

My drug money bought me lots of phony friends and
women;
Young and old men look up to me because of my drug
money (damn fools)
I got people wanting to dress like me, walk and talk like me
because of my drug money (again how foolish)

I have been all over the world because of my drug money;
I hang out with all kinds of famous people because of my
drugs and drug money;
I am the man because of my drug money;

I think about what my drug money has done to my life and
theirs nothing good to come out of it all;
My family won't accept me or my drug money;
I lost my wife and children because of my drug money;

I can't trust any body over this drug money
I have lost excellent jobs because of drug money
Why should I have to work when I can make over $5-
10,000 per day?

I set in my mind I will kill for my drug money
I guess that's why I have been shot for my drug money
I been to jail for my drug money
And this is why my funeral is being held today for my drug
money.

I'M IN PAIN:

The negative things that I do is destroying my soul I know this may sound strange but I am ready for a ultimate change I need to be free from negativity I pray God will forgive me and have mercy on my soul for all the times I blacked out and lost control.

I really don't want to sin anymore GOD help me I am weak I need strength instruct me on how to be a real man and how to live life the right way as I lay down to rest when I awake in the morning please bless me with the wisdom that I need to succeed.

Right now FATHER I surrender and put my life in your hands because I am in pain I can't go on doing the bad wicked things that I do break these evil chains off of me Take this pain away I'm tired of living as a liar, thief, a man who takes advantage of women abusing them mentally and physically I don't want to do that any longer.

Its like all I do is run from the truth run from my self because I do not enjoy the person I am at this time I know I am not asking for too much FATHER let me know you are I need to feel your warm loving touch So that this pain can go away.

Not Impressive:

Young boy on the block talking about he holding it down robbing dudes for they cellphones and weed do anything just to get a name create a rep dumb ass don't even know he caught a robbery charge for stealing homeboy phone now he mad in jail talking about the cat snitched how foolish you idiot you robbed him you played the hand and got dealt with.

It contradicts itself and I am not trying to condone but damn if you going to get money be about that spread for real you walk or ride a stolen bike and when you drinking from that bottle you didn't buy that bottle but you be the first to want to pop that bottle they homies by weed you the first to be like spark it up but you broke and you clown and everyone knows it it's a shame you don't realize it though.

Get it together young blood these streets will eat you alive you the type that will end up dead or up north over some bullshit lost in the system uneducated because you thought school was wack now you struggle for the rest of your life because you took shit for granted thinking it was all a game you was the nigga up north begging for bread and soap looking for handouts just like you do in the streets so tell me young blood who are you, because niggas in the street don't know you, who are you fam you have no identity.

Basically youngster you need to reevaluate your life restructure you entire being get educated in and out of the streets because at the end of the day the street corner you slanging and banging on is always going to be here but you will not don't be angry because I am kicking the truth you so blind to what's really shaking you just made a sale and didn't see the DT's on top of the roof.

My message to you youngsters and this may not apply to all of you man listen do the right thing the streets is not for anyone some survive some don't either way you look at it's a 50/50 chance you just better off getting your high school diploma go to college get a trade or if you built for it play the military but whatever you do make something positive out of yourself and be easy youngster.

Wish it didn't have to be like this:

Back in this dirty game things sure have changed no real hustlers around anymore so this is what I have to deal with a bunch of young knuckle heads well it is what it is I just really hope they stay out of my way because the anger that is inside of me will not hesitate to put one of them in a box.

Playing my position I see how these lames move and I'm not feeling it I pray I don't have to play these streets to long this clown over here thinking because he make a stack a week he doing something fucking fool you better of getting a job I make a stack selling oils and incents little homie its real out here guess you just don't know.

Those who love me tell me please don't take it to the street they want to preach and got a lot to say so my question to you is are you going to pay my bills feed my wife and daughter let's not get it twisted because we both know the answer to that so there's nothing you can tell me right now I got to hustle and get out this hole once things get better maybe I can walk away for good until then It is what it is.

My wife and others tell me to pray well I am all prayed out reading the bible going to church for me is played what I have been asking God to help me with and bless me with he is not hearing me my patience have run out so now I am back in the game and the animal in me is out this time around I am not playing any games who ever crosses me the wrong way will get buried the same day in the worst way I am prepared for the consequences I guess it's true like they say get down or lay down and I don't plan on laying down.

Seems like I was born without a chance just a black man trying to do right make something good of my life but I feel like where is this shit getting me I am still struggling and going through the everyday bullshit of trying to find a better way and nothing is happening so I have no choice but to take it to the street and make shit happen my criminal mind that was once put away has been unlocked reformed better than ever because I had time to learn from past mistakes and I am doing this alone no room for partners I am not trying to get knocked or rocked to sleep because of the jealous ones I don't need security I am good it's just me and my two guns Mack 11 and 9 millimeter hopefully I will never have to pull the trigger but If I do I guess it happened for a reason.

This shit is really whack but I got to sling this snow as much as I hate it must be done and I know I am wrong but it's not the first time I have done wrong charge it to the game I tried other options in every direction only to get no results not good ones any way so I am going to flow like I know and pray I don't get caught for the things I am doing because deep down inside I know I should be laying back chilling but I have to survive and get out this hole and make things better and if shoveling this snow is the wave then I am riding it to the bitter end.

My Beautiful Black People:

My people no longer understand the meaning of peace, love, happiness and respect it's sad to see another brother killing his fellow brother over a female, street corner and a color what has happened to us some say it's getting better but the truth is it is getting worse just the other day the young boy from down the block was arrested for snatching his own aunts purse and they say we are making progress it sure is hard to tell.

Ignorance is slowly killing our race this negativity we are living in is such a shame black men losing their lives to drugs, aids and violence sisters belittling their beautiful minds and bodies for cocaine until they have gone completely insane.

What not to do, are the words I ask you I am sure we know right from wrong we just choose to do wrong if we can living foul only thing we can expect to gain is pain and suffering if we don't change and come together we are all going to lose in the worse way;

Go ahead run in these streets like a crazy animal until the penitentiary or a bullet permanently paralyzes you;

Black on Black crime, will it ever stop no longer can I bear this captivity of my people being broken down by our own negativity.

Our Children:

For the children we must stop the violence
Who really wants their sons and daughters joining gangs growing
up to be sent to prison or to an early grave we are not being good
examples at all.

Everyday I see my the intelligence of my black brothers and sisters
so the question I ask is why do you keep selling your selves short I
know life is hard and sometimes you have to fight for those good
things that are positive but that's life it self.

I know from experience what living negative can do this is why I
choose to live a positive healthy life it seems as if drugs, gangs and
guns have taken over our communities negative music, movies,
and videos are destroying thousands of young minds.

It's sad to see 13 year olds throwing up gang signs and
disrespecting one another because of a color we must not Robb
them of their child hood or education they are innocent young
children so if you can't stop the violence and negativity for
yourselves at least do it for the children.

STOP THE GANG WAR:

I remember when the two of you used to be friends how you'll use
to play together, go to the same baby sitter, sleep at each others
house went to junior high school together shared clothes so how
could you let a color and negativity of money guns and the streets
take away your beautiful friendship.

Hate and death is what you now share because he represents red
and you rock blue was it ever really supposed to get this crazy look
how our communities have changed.

Innocent children are being killed getting caught in the cross fire,
who are you to determine who lives and dies, you are trapped in a
world of evilness, and ignorance its sad that you can't open your
eyes and realize the damage your doing to your selves and others.

What's it going to take for you to stop a sharp bullet or knife?
Do you truly know what a gangster is?
My definition of a Gangster is a man who does not kill a man for
colors money drugs or anything at all a real Gangster will learn to
reason now I know sometimes you can't always reason and things
happen but what we are doing today is uncalled for.

Further more I feel that if you're so Gangster you should be
providing a roof over your families head educating your sons and
daughters about the dangers of the street treating that lady of your
life like the queen she is.

Don't look for excuses to kill a person or to say this is why I gang
bang because there are many people who had it rough who found a
safe way out of the life of crime who was able to go a positive
route.

You young boys out there on the block call yourselves holding it
down being thugged out for your man but when shit hits the fan I
don't see your homie busting his gun or coming to bail you out of
jail.

Now look who is doing the time crying like a bitch because you
know you played your self about to do 33-life for shooting a cat
from the other side ask your self is losing your life to the system
really worth it.

Brothers and sisters too because you'll down just as well don't
justify the systems plan and trap your self off only for them to

WHO AM I:

I hate peace I hate higher power I hate any one who loves his fellow brother or sister to all who come in contact with me I wish you death and suffering.

I enjoy seeing Fathers and mothers crying filled with anger it thrills me to see your sweet children being carried away in a hearse and families torn apart.

I come into the minds of many but I am quicker to manipulate teenagers or those who are sincerely weak I have killed millions and am very pleased I'll sneak up on you when you least expect it I am in the blood of every race I have no love for Gods children I destroy communities, countries and house holds I am evil.

I love it when the bloods and crips kill one another and the Latin kings destroy the Ms 13 I don't care if innocent children lose their lives they should not have been in my way I destroy all that is good even as I speak to you right now I am planning a thousand more funerals.

I need more guns and knives in your children's hands I get a kick out of seeing your sons and daughters go to jail for the rest of there lives its my duty to make sure the rot in hell.

Its true I am very well hated and I always show up unexpectedly but you choose to have me so many have chosen me over reality and peace.

I thank the parents who are too busy getting high, out partying or just don't care at all to educate there children about me, you know those of you who let your children roam the streets at all hours of the night leaving them to fin for them selves feeling unloved

Pushing them into gangs, drugs, murdering people committing crimes and doing all sorts of negative things.

Yeah I know I'm just an evil son of gun SO WHAT am I am growing bigger than ever oh allow me to introduce myself my name is VIOLENCE you know me the one who causes a man to beat on his wife or your child to go out and rob and shoot someone because of a color or he feels his crew is better than the next clique.

Don't think I only target men didn't I mention before I destroy women too I love the pretty gullible ones they will do anything for me hurt anybody I tell them to I told you I can easily manipulate the weak and enjoy it bottom line is I'm the world's worst nightmare and I do not plan on leaving until all of you are dead or permanently suffering it's like they say on a man and woman's wedding day once you have me it is until death do us part no divorce no walking away I am violence and I will snatch your ass before you can blink your eye so you better beware.

So until we meet again oh and we will meet again I wish you families, men and women young and old eternal pain and suffering I am violence.

Table of Contents:

Chapter 1. Drugs Disease and Sex

5. Do you remember what happened last night?

6. What is my name?

7-8.Dad loves crack more than me

9-10. Temptation

11-12.Drugs killed mom and dad

13. for the mothers who are struggling

14. I'm dying

15. Mama you're killing me

16. Overdose

17. Two years clean

18. Mommy I am hungry

19. Chapter 2. Encouragement

20. for the ladies

21. it's up to us

22. Life saver

23-24 Time for a change

25. Use your mind for you not against you

26. Love my brother

27. Statistics

28. The woman

29. to my brothers

30. Not a good look

31. Be your best friend

32-33. when the sunrises

34. Chapter 3. Higher Power

35. A cry for help

36. Free us

37. God is good

38. I know God forgives

39. Acknowledgements

40. A mothers Love (My Beautiful mother)

41. to my father

42. Victoria and Payton

43. My love (Akeya Faith Jenkins) Now known as Akeya Robinson

44-50 thank you

51 chapter 4. My life what a journey it has been

52. about me

53. Cannot understand

54. Doing my best to move on

55. Fighting with the devil in my cell

56-57. to whom it may concern

58-60 Respect it

61. The night I thought I wanted to dies

62. three times

63. until you touch down

64. Chapter 5. Respect is what all children Deserve no matter what race they may be.

65. A friend that cares

66. Bad man

67. Black Butterfly

68. Untitled

69. Mr. Police officer

70. Questions and thoughts

71. Stop being selfish it's not all about you

72. Stop leaving your woman alone

73. Chapter 6. Romance The lover in me

74. after tonight

75. Black rain

76-77. Chocolate covered strawberries and cherries

78. Countless times

79. Empty without you

80. for my wife

81-82 give it to me

83. Hunting for love

84. Hypnotized

85. I'm getting in that

86. Just want to tell you

87. I want to be next to you

88. I want to know

89. Last night I heard you cry

90. When I close my eyes

91. My plan is to love you the best way I can

92. Secret Garden

93. Tonight I am going to be you love Maestro

94. Undressing you with my eye

95. Unstoppable

96. Whenever forever

97. When love is gone

98. Chapter 7 Street life and violence

99. Do you hear me crying?

100. Drug money

101. I'm in pain

102. Not impressive

103. Wish it didn't have to be like this

104. My beautiful black people

105. Our children

106. Stop the gang war

107-108 Who am I

I would like to personally thank all of my family and friends and people in general who support my book I hope that when you read my words that they touch your heart and you understand that my words will always and forever come from my heart. I do not write to offend anyone I write what I feel what I may know from experience or have seen I pray and hope that you will enjoy reading my words and continue to support me and the future thank you.

Donald David Robinson II